Foreword

This isn't easy. For most men, it's safe to say that it's also not easy to admit conflict with depression. This is a combination of self-reflection on my struggles with two failed marriages, choosing horrible partners, questioning my identity and the like. Some may call it a reflective memoir – you be the judge. My intention is to provide a portal to the emotional rollercoaster that I have experienced and to perhaps provide hope or a relative idea for both men and women struggling with the same issues. It is a direct reflection of a decade of betrayal, loss, highs and lows and a deep journey spiritually. In this, considering not only the world around me, but also the burning desire to thrive. Most of these writings are not directed at any one person and the names have been removed to protect those involved. Pages have been left intentionally blank for your reflection. It is my purest intention for those of you suffering, to have an outlet, encourage you to choose the right partner, to have love and a sense of security in your life.

-Love to All,

Ben

Who I am

I came from nothing. I had a mother who was still searching for herself and was stuck in purgatory over the loss of her mother at a young age. I had a stepfather who wanted me to be something more than I was…and I couldn't see it. I went to my beloved music to escape. Spending countless hours lamenting through my drug to find myself. I had beautiful friends to show me what life was…thank God for them! Out of the wreckage I survived. I had to take control…because to me it was between death and rejection; both had a sweet aroma. I have lived my life to spite everything anyone said I couldn't do. I have overcome every barrier. I have created myself. Yes…am I proud. Yes, I am self-righteous. Yes, I pat myself on the back. I have built my own fortress out of nothing…I WILL NOT APPOLOGIZE. I have bled to be a father to my children and wasn't a "step-dad" I was the "dad who stepped up". I have suffered to provide for my family. I have fought for my country. I have given confidence to thousands of people. I know what hell is and have seen/lived it. But I've spent 43 years finding out who I am…so here it is:

I am the bitter taste of jealousy
I am the cunning sting of malice
I am the taring of emotional wallpaper
I am the tantrum throwing child
I am the coward who kicks the weak
I am the executioner of words
I am the judge of logic
I am the bite from the hound
I am the whipping post
I am the false prophet
I am revenge
I am the arrogance of the self-starter
I am the fire of the driven
I am the lost child in the market
I am the mouse in a maze
I am the manipulative Svengali
I am the foot on your throat
I am the sugar from the bowl
I am the labor of love.
I am enough
I just "Am."

The Betrayal

Amazing what hasty decisions are made on a whim. How unfortunate sacred words get played like one string on a battered guitar…the bitter sound that is off key. I have found myself a victim of betrayal. Am I blind to assume that the misfortune of the world seems to affect only me? Am I the sap that drips from the wounded tree with the words "We are forever" who believes that love in its most simple state is a utopia for the blind?…I must, I am married to betrayal. What pleasure lies in the fields of torn emotion and sorrow? The illusion that faithfulness is something only the clergy do. I am torn….ripped apart from every facet that was real in the memory of love. My heart forgave the first time without a second thought of the meaning of repentance was to be. Then the wrath came…I was struck with the tearing of my soul…the flesh ripped away like a savage dog from a carcass. In four days you somehow found the Holy Grail in cheap words of encouragement to forsake the one who gave you a reason to exist. After months of pondering, you had an epiphany that somehow, the vicious text really didn't mean what I interpreted. Slowly, I began to rebuild from the ashes… A twelve-year masterpiece sand castle that had been destroyed by a juvenile bully. And like a child you were burned by the candle that was cheap lip service…did you learn? Months went by and I was beginning to have hope of the cheap thrill again…love. Then out of innocent curiosity, I began to slowly be crucified with a telescope that magnified the horror of the ages….betrayal. The words set fire to my veins…..my blood boiled with vengeance…I fought to the death to keep my hands from crushing the bones of someone who was already dead. Dead to her husband, dead to her children, dead to the world…the queen of "self" had taken her thrown with war-like force. The cheapness of it all…like reading pages of a ripe smut magazine….and I shared a bed with it…betrayal. Cheap thrills that ruined the craftsmanship of a master builder. Like a fool I will forgive you again…until next time…when the wrath of righteousness will shred what's left of a soulless demon…you too will learn how to rebuild from the ashes…except selfishness will keep you from seeking the material to build. I am the ship's hull…the centerline of strength. I will set sail again…I will have the open water as a solace from you and your scurvy called ……betrayal.

The Prodigal Returns

The wheels spin rapidly as I rush to return. All the while, I am captivated by the smallest things I have forgotten. The pleasant smells of fresh cut grass and lavender fill the air as an old tune plays on the radio. Where did it all go? I've spent way too much time chasing a façade that was never there. Trying to love someone when all I felt was disappointment when it wasn't reciprocated. Chasing a white rabbit with a dollar bill tied to its tale was my life's mission – I have forgotten who I am. And just when the thought hits me…a lyric takes my memory to a better place in my life. The peaceful calm of the morning has reminded me and my senses of the place of my birth. No city madness…just nature speaking with the loudest peace that I have been in desperate need of for far too long-without realizing it. As many years have passed trying to leave this place, I've come to realize that this has always been home.

Above All

In the midst of a tragic end, I have been left with nothing. On one hand, it's a freedom that I have needed to be released to for so long. However, even after taking my livelihood and soul from me, she still has the nerve to ask, "How are you doing? How is your health." This superficial play on words has left me at a stalemate. For what I'd usually pay no attention to and consider it small talk or maybe even something to raise my temper, I now am stuck in a purgatory of confusion. Not so much that the simple questions have left me to be angry or not, but more "Why?" than anything. She never seemed to mind stripping me of my soul, which was my children or the material things that I worked so hard at achieving. So, I have to wonder why she would care if I were still breathing. My answer of "why do you care?" left me with a dead ring tone. My instinct told me to call her back, but somehow, I knew not to…she'd win and the juvenile little fits that are so familiar would only spark bad memories. Lately I feel close to God, or rather – God is close to me. I wasn't trying to be rude…but somehow it was mistaken that way. My patients have been truly put to the test with an angry ex-mother-in-law hanging the phone up on me while I was answering a very important question to my angelic daughter. The only lifeline that I had to my beautiful kids was cut short due to self-righteous greed and inconsideration. Even after a small stint with helpless rage…he [God] was there to embrace me. Maybe it's just that this whole experience has caused me to truly acknowledge God for who he is. My God, amazing creator and intimate friend, you really do have a place for me even though I am totally confused as to

what your plan is for me…I long to seek your favor.
God, show me what you want from me and guide me
in the right way. I need you, I need your forgiveness,
and I need your compassion and understanding. Be
the God who pulls me out of this pit and rescue me
from myself.

Science of God

No matter whom we are within this society- we answer to the science of God. When we strip ourselves away from our socio-economic standing – our cultures- our trends – our things…. we become nothing more than another element in the periodic table of the divine.

(After holding niece Hope)

Thinking of Zachery

In nothing more than raw emotion, I feel the tearing of my heart as I relive tragedy as I let my son from my arms. His tears and reaching hands left a dark emptiness upon me. Have I forsaken him? Did I not fight hard enough like a hero should? So, I sit gripping the earth, my tears dampening the soil and all I can remember is his touch and desperate voice. Will he ever understand a father's love? The sand of hope falls between my fingers and I begin to bleed. I am a prisoner but, yet I stand free in an open field feeling the burn of the aftermath. My thoughts are filled with all I've done and the tumbling of useless things – like watching trinkets fall from their shelves. You can have all that's left…the scraps of an amazing life. We have been born from clay and water only to leave with ashes divided. In this life there are things that even pills can't fix. Life is a mystery…like music, there are only seven notes between rubble and a masterpiece…its all how you fit it together. So, I let him go again to open the wounds that seem to never heal. My sweet boy, I will forever suffer the consequences of your sad heart. I will lay sleepless wondering your thoughts. I will learn of your life through pictures and will remain broken for what I have done.

Erin (Ireland)

As the song of the pipes play, I struggle with the swelling of tears. It is as if you can hear the breaking of a heart. Maybe it's the sound of mine breaking. A true blend of melodic cries mixed with beauty. I miss the damp grass beneath my feet – the sound of the night at my back door- the cozy comfort that the Irish countryside provides and the smell of the air after the rain. Why did I leave? Sometimes I wonder if somewhere in those hills she is waiting for the fog to clear and come running to me from the mist.

Circle of Cedars

I remember you…the feeling of the moist soil beneath my feet. I remember the breeze upon my soft skin as a boy. Who were you? Are you the remains of a fairy tale land that we never knew? Look at the bark torn from your majestic foot…the timeless nature of your body…sacred like much of what I can remember…you are me. Oh, if only you could speak to me…the images that you would explain long before man consumed the hillside with greed. I can stand in the middle of this strong circle and feel the safety of you all around me. What did the brush-strokes of God feel like when he painted you here on the mountain? I can smell your spirit in the air. Man has failed…man has failed. We cut you down just to shred you to pieces to fill the bedding of the mongrels. In all of this, you do not complain…you are humble…you stand strong. So, I will sit against you for a while…breathing you in…and you embrace me. My circle of cedars…my friends…I'm sorry…If I hide you will you share the same stories to the generations after me? I will remain true to self, standing strong when people just want a piece of me as a trophy. I will stand strongly silent until the cutting chain strips my life away from me. I will take you with me…my heaven will have you there to love…and the lips of God will kiss you in the morning and my hands will care for you forever.

Angel for the Broken

    I remember you sitting there so quietly absorbing everything I had to say and how I found it hard to focus just because you were there looking back. I tried to tell myself to look past you, but I couldn't – I was drawn to you. Every word that rolled off your lips seemed to have greater meaning to me -like it was a language that I could completely understand. Beyond this, you always said the right thing in which ever context you put it -I was beside myself. Your life stories I grabbed and wanted to hold onto forever -like the greatest book ever written but I only had it for a short time, then it was gone. "Gone" is a hard thing to accept but for some reason you always appeared at the right time…and I can't explain it – it was like having a guardian angel. Is that what you are? An Angel? My realist perspective has always caused me to never put much value in dreams, fate, destiny or even angels -but somehow you prove it wrong. Am I not the non-conformist realist that I thought I was? What are you doing to me? Should I fear you? Please -I'm shattered, scared, torn, bleeding and wasting away. You should probably stay back because my disease of sorrow could consume you too. As I walked to the door of a childhood refuge and saw that the home was empty -so was I. Then from a thousand miles away, you responded with a simple message -I couldn't believe it -you were with me again. How do you do that? I rounded the corner and I was in paradise. Did you guide me? Everything around me reminded me of you. The trickling waterfall reminded me of your spirit -free flowing, beautiful and calm. I only got to embrace you once, but I remember how wonderful you smelled, but it wasn't the right time to tell you. The breeze brushed the flowers and softly pressed itself against me, and there you were. I wonder if you even know what you are to me -and if you did, would you understand? Sometimes the simplest words go unsaid because they don't carry the impact of the feeling. I believe that you would understand, but my insecurities keep me from you. If you are my angel, then I am humbly glad.

Hallmark

Amid total chaos, you stand softly gentle to the things that torment your heart. With a beautiful smile upon your face you reach out a hand of kindness while others dare to through daggers towards you. In this human life, you resemble all that is good and pure of heart, yet it goes unnoticed by those who act like vultures with their unnecessary laziness, selfishness and greed. I sit from a distance thinking about you and wishing I could strategize a way to invade your life and rid you of these things.   The warrior rages inside me only to realize that my hands are bound. I then realize that in my combative emotions that you would remain the calm one. I am reminded that gentleness and love will conquer all and the beauty of your smile is a blinding light upon me and I gain my freedom. In our struggles we find that a strong hand to hold and shoulder to lean on will save us from the fall of whatever our troubling enemy is. You are my rock and my safety; without you I am wounded and abandoned. With you, I find strength and happiness, courage to persevere, laughter and joy in simplicity….I Love You.

Torch

Cut me deeper so I can bleed through my own conscience.

Chew up my past and spit it back in my face.

Let the last words from your mouth curse me till the end of my days.

Pound your assumptions into my chest.

Tell me all that I'm "not" to satisfy all that "I am" to you.

Rebuke the divine and deny all the miracles you've witnessed.

Rip the pleasures from my hands and burn my sincerity.

Call me shallow and turn a blind eye to my depth.

Say I'm cold and throw away my warm heart.

Burn me to ashes till my existence is soot.

Feral

I would be lying if I said that thought of you didn't cross my mind from time to time. More so lately, you are a distant memory. Oh, the days of contemplation of what I'd do to you if the opportunity arose that you and I would meet each other face to face, alone and no one else is around. Knowing every inch of your home from years of carful observation. Knowing exactly how to destroy you slowly. To present myself as I warned you right to your face without any support of your would-be brotherhood. You arrogantly and ignorantly bought into a lie. You had the audacity to challenge me to the point of walking into my home and sleeping with my wife while I was there. You do realize that the only reason you're still breathing is because I refuse to engage in violence around children? Now, you are idiot number 4. I bailed you out either directly or indirectly by way of supporting her. I fed you, rescued you, unknowingly let you stay in "our" vacation spot and even spared your life in ways you can't possibly imagine. Now, and through your actions, she has now left you. I showed temperance toward you when you decided to challenge me in front of my family by punching me through my car window. Did you realize I had a loaded gun next to me? Did you realize that I have a killer nerve? You've dodged a reckoning more than once with me. I then sit and mull over these encounters with you. Boys like you will never become men. You've been enabled to be a reckless juvenile. Oh, how you've danced with death and didn't realize it. Then, through wisdom, I have overcome my anger with you. Vengeance isn't mine anymore and I've let go of the rage. You will be met by someone whose patience runs much shorter than mine. Your self-image of being a warrior/outlaw will be met swiftly by a jaw-breaking punch of reality. I wish you all the best little boy. Though I doubt you'll survive long, my hope is one day you can become something of worth.

ROBERTS

Stolen Valor

You've been the thorn in my side for years. The very cause of what took a beautiful/loving relationship and wreaked havoc on pure love. I often wonder what disease has eaten your brain. My education, experience and world travels have never encountered anything like you…ever. Who you are would even baffle the likes of Young and Freud. Here you are, a small-town kid who raised his right hand to join a cause. In doing so, you were mediocre at best. So much to the fact that your superiors pawned you off as much as they could until you played the "broken" card. Meanwhile, you had a wife who loved you. She kept the home front stable while you were off eating government issued ice cream and taking pictures of your "little private" in a port-a-john. She prayed for you while you killed her spirit with your words and actions. She put her life on the line just to satisfy your lust – yet you sought pleasure from the trailer park. She gave you an opportunity to be a father to a little boy that needed you, but you chose to abuse him. She bore you a daughter who is so beautiful and full of life – yet you tortured her by slandering her mother, allowing another woman to hurt her and you stood by and did nothing. You had a responsibility to her, your daughter and your step-son. I found her in the nick of time and trying to hold her so tightly that everything you broke within her would miraculously fuse back together…it never did. You devote your life to bullying. You suck your teeth and laugh after demolishing the innocence of children. You literally brag and boast about driving the broken to take their own life. Yes, you've temporarily gotten away with murder. Yes, I just called you a MURDERER! I know it and so do you. When will you learn hero? You act like the world owes you something for your service...but the only thing you served was your psychological need for mayhem. Yes Sarge, you still owe your country something. Yes Sarge, you need to learn what integrity is. Yes Sarge, you know nothing of valor. Yes Sarge, you don't deserve children, comfort or a home all paid for by the American public. Yes Sarge, you're a bigot. Heroes are faceless.   They ask for nothing in return for doing their duty. You will be the one your own dog doesn't come to because, even to it, you are nothing.

Stockholm Syndrome

It's a hard pill to swallow when suddenly you wake up only to realize that you have been taken hostage by an obligatory terrorist. There's no other way to describe it. I've been tortured for years with countless interrogation when I did nothing wrong. Meant to believe I was the cause of the war that was waged by her evil doings. To sympathize with the enemy and believing the stupid rhetoric that justifies her actions. The torture that literally had me on death's door more than once and had me psycho-evaluated just to keep my livelihood in place. The livelihood that provided you safety, love and your basic Maslow needs. Then just like the black-masked others, you sell your agenda on social media and give praises to your Gods who condone your actions and give you justification. Just like a shocking bucket of ice...I woke to clarity. I realized my value and my worth. You think you're the first woman who tried to kill me? Hahaha...get in line Jezebel! I now envision a mirror in my hand and every time you speak ill of me...I mentally send it right back to your wicked shell. You are a fraud. Flippantly false advertising what you sell as a Godly woman.

Sisyphus

The sound of a memory consumes my mind –
the gentle lyrics of a timeless song explains the
discontent of my heart. I sit and write page after page
of relentless turmoil…a heart collapsing yet the words
fail to express fully what I'm feeling. Though the
numbness has subsided, the confusion of feeling now
takes the stage. In one way…I'm so overwhelmed….in
another, I'm so empty…as hard as I push to recognize,
it's unfamiliar. I've let go of all the egotist attributes
that are damaging to a man's character…but in doing
so, have I released the strength of my gender? Am I
falling apart? I feel like I'm fighting blindfolded…not
knowing where the punches are coming from…not
knowing how to defend myself. I start swinging at
nothing hoping to connect, but fatigue is setting
in…and I'm beginning to lose. What does it mean to
truly overcome? Tell me what perseverance really is
and how long must you go on. Am I just Sisyphus?-
continually trying to push the rock over the
mountain…but always getting crushed by it when I get
close to the top?

Post Detonation

It's like a close proximity explosion going off. That ginormous **BOOM!!!** only to be softened by an overwhelming ringing in the ears…then total silence. You struggle to find your composure but are disoriented with a feeling of "what just happened?" Years and thousands of words lamenting your heart and thoughts now disintegrated into nothing. Two years of threats, constant emotional back and forth, "I love you-s" mixed with fueled feelings of hate….it is all over. Tomorrow, I will wake to clarity and the realization that the covenant that I took will now be relinquished as if it never happened. My step-children will just know me as "Ben" no longer "Dad." No thank you-s for contributions, financial help, gifts or great memories made. No apologies from her even still – nor closure for the unknown or undefined…not even a good bye. I will wake up alone again like always…she wakes up to someone new…like always. The war is over and neither surrendered but gave up fighting and walked away. Through the trauma, bleeding and recovery, I will be a better version of who I know I am. I will still pray for her and yes, still love her just on a different level. I hope her wandering will lead her to the greener grass she's always searched for. I hope she puts down the torches she's lit that have burned so many bridges. I hope her mouth speaks only the truth and never spills slander to build a false agenda. I hope her heart grows a love for the divine and lives by the code that she says is her anthem. I hope that she will be the amazing and available mother I know she is and not let relationships hinder her bond with her children. I hope that whomever she chooses will adore the children as much as I do. I pray her reality will become something of real life and not a façade over social media. I hope she finds value in her personality not her sexuality to attract others. I hope the light always shines on her and that her path will be the road less traveled. May the silencing blast change the course of history and destroy the miserable cycles for us both.

The Crow

In the dusk hours I hear you call from on top of the dead oak tree like the soul of a witch chanting incantations. You represent all that is ugly in this world. You are the reaper of humanity...you are the thief of souls. Every black feather of your down represents an evil deed you've done to destroy me. Even now I can still feel your talons tearing apart my ears. You are not a scared one...every defense you have cleverly figured out. I tried to protect my garden and still you feed on what is rightfully mine. You pecked away my life just to feed the gluttony of your fiendish appetite. You spoke the unspeakable just to steal the sweet taste of joy from my mouth. You are a robber...a wretched scavenger. You enjoy feeding on the dying just before the heart stops to feel the body shake one last time before you leave it for the rats...I overcame your pecking...I overcame your reaping...I've caught you stealing and I will make you pay...either in this life or the next...the last thing you will ever hear is a gunshot rushing through a barrel of truth. You will fall from your perch only to be fed upon by the others you once co-conspired with...until that day...caw away...caw away...your days are numbered -as I foresee your end.

The Question

I sit and watch the black letters spread across the myriad of white yet I struggle to find meaning in anything. It never seems to fail that when I have the time to breathe, I have time to think. Thinking is a dangerous game lately with the cyclones of reality swarming all around me. I do welcome the reality, but not being able to grasp it is nothing more than an exhausting challenge. Where did I release my spirit? When did the acceptance from a lover drive away my identity? I am patient…I have been kind…I do not envy…I am love. I suppose there is no use for struggling to reach something I can't grasp. I gave her the essence of what makes me human…it wasn't enough. I thought I was an anchor. I look at myself in the mirror and ask, "What have you become?" The mirror says, "You have aged, and your face shows many scars as much as you try to doctor it with words." Will I find her out there? Someone who is undeniably real and loving? Will I have to prove anything to her? Will I have to deal with the emotional, maniacal fits? Will I be enough? – Scars and all?

The Search for Eldorado

I've been completely blindsided by so many emotions lately that I have absolutely no idea who I even am anymore. It's sad because I have always thought that I had myself figured out to a certain degree and now, once again in this lifetime, I'm depressed. But why? She has said "this was your choosing." Yes, I chose her, her flaws and to stick around. However, what is it truly about her that keeps me taking her back constantly? It's beyond frustrating because every logical piece of evidence would have any other man running in the opposite direction…then I'm the one who goes running directly to the inferno knowing full-well that I will be consumed and burned. I see past photos of myself and reflect on how happy I was…. especially during the Mod-Team days. I was outgoing, making a very comfortable living, had an amazing girlfriend etc. Then it all went to hell in a hand basket….WHY? I couldn't commit to Jn the way that she needed me and I couldn't accept what appeared to be her mediocrity. All she wanted was to get married and have children…was that really so hard to give her?...looking back now?...No….it wouldn't have been. Then off to T. She was absolutely amazing…but there was secrets I was unaware of and probably dodged a bullet. Hands down some of the greatest passion I ever had and whenever I wanted it. She was the first person I dated too since Jd who actually took care of me like a good partner. I honestly don't think she was divorced yet nor over her ex-boyfriend…it's a mystery to this day. Even so, I was very hurt when we split. Then there was S….which was the start to the train wrecks. She was pretty no doubt and the affection in the beginning made up for the simple fact that she was a felon and from an extremely unfitting background. This was the start to me putting up with extreme toxicity from women. Somehow, she planted a seed or virus into my mind that didn't allow me to let go of her. By the grace of God…I made it out. I wasn't looking for anyone and met K out of nowhere. Even though there was a pureness and innocence to our relationship, it just wasn't meant to be….but I am grateful to her for instilling the confidence I needed to rid myself of S. Then out of nowhere, my co-worker M introduced me to Y. It was like getting struck by lightning. I immediately fell in love with her to the point of accepting flaws and unacceptable things beyond what any human being should ever have to deal with. Countless cheating, flirting, getting pregnant, slander, stalking, alienation, creating enemies….and the list goes on and on. So many times, I have thrown my hands up in frustration or in true helplessness to God and begged for help. I have relentlessly prayed for this woman…I have selflessly loved her…I have raised and provided for her and her children…and I have been emotionally trampled by her almost daily. So again….what is it that has kept me from saying goodbye to her permanently? The only conclusion I have found is simply Bb. She will use that beautiful baby to control me at any cost. She can stipulate who I can have my own daughter around just by virtue of giving birth to her -never mind the simple fact that she can play house with whomever she pleases and thus screwing up now her third child. What it really boils down to is the simple fact that she doesn't want to her children exposed to someone who is actually better than her. She's a "good" mother no doubt, but her decision making has caused permanent damage to the kids....even Bb. So I guess I am protecting Bb with all that I have and lord forbid that a woman actually love her and be loving towards her father giving her a sense of normalcy, stability and something to look up to. Likewise, my family adores Bb and wants so badly to be close to her also knowing that the possibility of a life-long relationship with her is grim. Then, just like evil clockwork, Y had zero power. So she stripped me of my happiness in one final blow. She may as well have taken a loaded gun and shot my daughter point blank right in front of me....instead, she shot my soul. I haven't seen my beloved since. The worst part is that I know she's out there...still waiting for her daddy. No matter who she's forced to believe is her father...we both know it's me. So Y was right "there are some things worse than death" she said as she was posturing this in my world. But Y, I will not satisfy you....rather, I will use your own words and let that set in – "There's a special place in hell for people like you."

Multiple Realities

So many things still left to the unknown. Things that cause extreme anxiety...especially in the morning. To know everything, but also know nothing - all in the same lapse of time. 5 years of questioning my own value and worth. Desperately trying to balance my sanity between thankless jobs, a dying marriage and no emotional support. Seeing images of myself and not even recognizing who I am anymore. I have become faceless with no identity. My joy comes from a daughter (and children) who love(s) me relentlessly and I don't know from one day to the next when she'll be plucked from my loving heart -the very thought nearly kills me. I scrape by barely and dodge financial bullets every single day. All while trying to be calm and loving towards anyone who will accept it from me....when all I want to do is self-detonate. I'm trying to walk as far away from my own darkness, but it pulls at me like a drug to a junky. I want blood. I want to torture those that have hurt me or my children. I want vengeance but it isn't mine to take.

( )

So this is the calm after the storm? I wait to anticipate the sky to collapse upon me…but there is nothing but the smell of scented candles and taste of wine. So, this is what it's like to be empty? Running around in a round room searching for corners? I am numb…I feel nothing…what is left of me? I'm pondering my existence. Is it better to be out of an uncaring world? Where is the launching pad? Did I leave a legacy? Did I make an impact? -what do I leave behind besides incredible children? I feel helpless…bound by guilt that has been placed upon me by her. I'm struggling to find meaning in anything. The food has no taste anymore…the wine has more satisfaction visually than of drinking value. My music sits unfinished because my mind cannot create anymore. My bed is uncomfortable trying to hold a pillow to take place of a lover and my words are more gibberish than ever and an incredible repeat of each other…Master of all creation…what are you waiting for? Have I not suffered enough??? End this…bring me happiness in small packages…is that asking too much? I have lost my ability to smile…I'm not even sure what emotion is anymore…I've become cold. My passion has become a studio of ransacked art. I can't even stand to hear myself breathe and words fall apart as I try to express myself in writing. Once a fighter now I am humbly forfeiting. I'm finished.

A Fond Memory

Behind four walls, I scratch away at what seems to be the essence of boredom. I search for something to spark an interest, but I'm struggling to maintain. I try to use my imagination and squeeze to remember fond memories – like holding my little girl in the Caribbean ocean as the storm engulfed us. I remember the water being like a drawn bath and the raindrops splashing against the tide onto my lips…I could taste the salt. The storm drew the fragrance of hibiscus into the air and the sounds of the rainforest engulfed the area like a dominant verb. While pondering this, the wind begins to blow outside this cell and I stop to have a look as a storm arrives overhead. It adds emphasis to the memory of that day. Suddenly, my feelings of boredom are changed to a peaceful quiet and I'm relaxed and happy.

Alissa

I have loved you a million lifetimes. The perfect manifestation of love in the flesh. From the second you opened your eyes, you reached out for my finger and have been there and in my heart ever since. You have always been wise. Your loving nature has forced you to take on emotional responsibilities so much bigger than even your elders could possibly imagine. I have so many wonderful memories of you and like a flash…I was gone. My availability has been less than what a father should have been – yet you persevered. I am working aimlessly to be something of worth to you by grasping the man I was to the man I am and will be to you. I hope that you know that a day has never past that I didn't think of you constantly. That little baby who would sit on my lap pounding piano keys, would sit on your bed next to me while I played you songs on the guitar. That little ringlet-haired angel that didn't want to let go of me when I came back from deployments and the little person that it broke my heart to ever leave. The intelligence of a philosopher who has taught even me so much about life and the world around us. The bold little lady whose individuality is second to none. I don't deserve you. Now you're a woman. Though my presence has been distant. You are the very proof that grace exists. You will do much bigger things than I can even imagine. You are my daughter, my first-born and my heart – as I told you as a child, "I can never live without my heart."

Legacy

We are the DNA of Noah - trusted by God to rebuild after he destroyed humanity.
- The children of Pharos, Caesar and Kings
- The builders/destroyers of Empires
- The very breath of greatness and evil

Yet we toil with earthly things:
- Greed
- Power
- Vanity
- Lust
- Entitlement
- Materialism
- Honesty
- Vengeance

Have we forgotten the footprints of our history?

Are we so meek that we can't harness the power of God and our ancestors to win battles over our trivial, yet miniscule adversaries?

We are the very greatness that inspired God to create us in his image.

We have unfathomable/supernatural strength given to us if we just ask and accept it.

We can grow in happiness if we just see the possibilities.

And goodness will ALWAYS triumph over evil....always.

Too Close to the Tide

He runs just as fast as his little feet will carry him to the beach with his plastic pail and shovel to create a masterpiece of grand proportions. His chubby little hands work as fast as they can to scoop and mold the sand into an unbreakable fortress. The more he builds, the more the tide returns to the shoreline. Finally, he stands proudly to show any willing person that he is finished…just then; a wave breaks and ruins his labor. I found myself reflecting on my own life. For so long I have tried to build too close to the tide. My efforts destroyed by some bullying wave or being crushed by a selfish act. As I approach the little man and wipe away his crocodile tears, I gently pick him up and take a few steps back and help him rebuild. Tears turned into direction and a sad little boy became the master of his world again. Maybe I should do the same, take a few steps back and rebuild paying closer attention to what is around me…especially the crashing waves.

(Inspired by Zach in Jamaica)

Declan

You were never mine. I waited anxiously knowing that you soon would take over our world and like your siblings, my heart. You are perfectly designed. Our connection is something that hardly anyone understands, yet we get each other without even saying a word. I watch you grow and grow. The sweet innocence that you have and loving heart towards anyone you ever meet. You display joy in everything and have a rhythm of your own. I love watching you have little moments of happiness where you will wake up from a dead sleep just to dance and sing to your favorite songs. You are the one when I'm having a hard day that looks at me and says "Daddy, you're beautiful" or "Daddy, you're my favorite." Sweet daughter, you are what makes me beautiful and gives me the power to secure your happiness in this lifetime. I will fight to ensure that the cruelty of this world, our poor decisions and now the separation of us, never breaks your heart. Like the others, I want to preserve your innocence never you knowing the things that have shattered my heart. I hope that over time and as you grow that you will always truly see me regardless of what people may say to you. I will always be your Dad no matter how many may try to take my place. I will hold you forever in my heart and in my arms. Sing little one....sing!

See Through

So often I struggle with who we are within the human race. I find myself pondering the countless and often trivial, yet transparent masks people wear. More often than not, I notice that people will exhaust themselves at trying to convince me that they are someone else. Maybe they are trying to be more attractive….maybe they are trying to be stronger, maybe they are trying to prove wisdom….maybe they are trying to prove their independence. On one side of the pane, they are who you want them to see and yet, on the other side, they are truly broken and often confused. Oh the masses of the mask, I can see through your plastic disguise and recognize a thief when I see it. Stop trying to steal favor, stop trying to prove your wisdom- recognize who you really are….be proud, be honest and mercy and love will surround you and your minions. Never fear the truth….love what you've become regardless of circumstances and know that fear is weakness in confidence.

One Fallen Petal

As I was walking, I saw a fallen petal of the most extraordinary kind. I picked it up and held it in my hands as he sits and sucks his teeth from the blood he's drawn from your soul – like a criminal who got away with vileness unimaginable. You sit shivering in the corner all huddled and terrified as he sits and smirks. I stand outside the window and begin to transform. My demons begin to raise my temperature with the flames of hell. My emotions flow from every vein and clinch my fists. What was a kind and outspoken nature has become the reckoning for this bottom feeder and suddenly I am in control. My hands have become silent messengers of pain. I grip his throat and feel his pulse wither as a thousand-mile stare freezes his heart. How could he harm you? I would venture to say that he didn't even value his own life let alone you. You were crafted by God's own hands and therefore, you are a miracle. The waves of anger have now turned to a calm rest. I place my coat around you and offer you my hand. Do you trust me? I assure you that all men are not equal, and this parasite has now become the compost to a beautiful flower. I will give you everything you need to flourish and grow, and I will show the world how breathtaking you truly are.

The Pendulum

Oh, how the pendulum swings-back and forth with no attempt at stopping...A series of motion wielding the wonder of where the start and end establishes themselves - In a way, it speaks well of our existence. Yes, we know where it begins and ends...but most of us do not choose when either one happens. I speak more of life as a series of events we experience. We might be fortunate to see the swing coming at us and brace ourselves....but often not. After impact, we feel the weight being released only to come back again with the same force we just experienced. We can say the same of turmoil, love, relationships....life. Oh, how the pendulum swings- people say that everything happens for a reason. The pendulum swings with great precision and its accuracy is the same every time...eternal...for a reason. Its purpose is to place time in our lives...it maintains a swing that moves the arms of our eternal clock...back and forth, to give us the brush strokes of the wonder of living....oh how the pendulum swings.

Beyond Beautiful

I've walked the shores of the most beautiful beaches; I've climbed the Alps. I've swam the blue lagoons and I've soared the canyons. I wandered the scorching Arabian deserts and I've trampled through the snows of Greenland. With my own two eyes I have seen the unexplainable. My hands have created both life and death. My mouth has spoken both blessings and curses. I've been so many things in this life…but out of all my over-comings…I could not overcome my loneness…until now. My heart has been shattered but has found something more than my eyes have seen and my hands have touched…something beyond beautiful. You've breathed life into my world. The very sight of you completely changes all that my senses know as familiar. Your eyes pierce through the fog and see right into the depths of me where the things of my life have been hidden. A simple touch from you sparks internal warmth that has been neglected for over a decade and draws me into you. I hold you and the scent of your hair reminds me of the flower fields of Holland or the hibiscus of the Caribbean. The sweet taste of your kiss causes me to forget who I am in this world and puts me into a timeless moment where it is only you and I. Your gentle voice brings me peace and calms the storms of turmoil in my mind. Every aspect of what makes you whole is something that has become beyond beautiful. Beyond anything in this life that I consider amazing. Beyond the unexplainable…your impact in my life is proof that God is listening.

Hype

To be told "you don't deserve to be happy" is a devastating blow. I have given my entire life to those who have, in turn, spat in the face of the most sincere/giving heart. I have gone without the spoils of my labor simply to provide to ungrateful takers. What is my magnetism to women like this? I am far from perfect. I understand my short-comings and am not only embarrassed, but also ashamed of the hurt I may have cause someone else. I have spent a fair amount of time repenting to those who I felt the need to make emends with. With all this, it is laughable. My father in his frustration said, "It doesn't have to be this way" – he was right and I exited the situation when the timing was right. Happiness is the ability to choose how you feel. I have wasted years of my life seeking happiness through other people. People who spoke impacting words but had no meaning either in the literal sense or through actions. I have been told "You can't survive alone." The point in this is that I have been alone forever. I, as well as even they, deserve happiness. However, my definition comes from within and through a faith in a higher power. Though I pride myself in being able to self-sustain, I will refuse to be dictated by the selfish. I will establish boundaries with those who need them. I will be kind even to my enemies not because they deserve it – but because it's right. I will overcome the doubters like I have my whole life. I will love myself first, then, when the time is right, she will present herself and I will love her deeply as I was made to do.

The Fro

We were just two rogues in the same room. Two defiant "anti-system" young men who had a passion for music and didn't play the local "political" game. We were thick as thieves. Being raised in a strict family atmosphere caused us both to rebel together. You were of age and use to sneak me beer and cigars. We'd play video game hockey for hours and always enjoyed a great take and back pizza and Monday night football. Then, like a brick falling out of the sky, we found a deeper focus. We became stronger and we lit up our world with a message and music. Spending several days with gear hanging out of the sun roof of your two-seat car going to rehearsal. Like true Rock Stars, we'd always load up on the dollar menu before rehearsals or a show. We hit the road together a lot. You never abandoned me. Even after a life decision that would take me around the world, you always made sure I was never alone. Marriage and careers have kept us busy and a significant distance didn't afford us a lot of time to see each other. Then out of nowhere, you called one day when the start of my dark ages began. Somehow, you've always felt when something wasn't right in my universe. You reached out to me when I had nothing left and told this lost man to "come home." You and your wife selflessly gave me a reason to live and allowed me the time I needed to heal. We have been family since day one. We have watched the other thrive and lifted the other up in our failures. There is truly nothing better in this world than knowing your best friend breathes the same air. That dude that has been your travel buddy, watched you make a fool of yourself, consulted you when you had no one, gave his unjudged wisdom and took you in when you had nothing. That man who has unbelievable talents that you've watched grow and mature for decades. That no matter the span of time that has gone, a conversation picks up where it left off. That man who considers you more family than his own blood. That man who knows more about you personally than even you do. That man who will square you away when you're on the wrong path…and you gladly listen and follow his lead. That man who you've celebrated victories with and bowed your head in reverence during tremendous loss. That man to whom you've never thought it improper to say, "I love you, man." ….and deeply meant it. I'd tread the depths of hell for you just to give you a high-five my dear brother. These are just simple words on paper and they will never relay the amount of gratitude I have towards you and your family. No matter where you are in this world, you just say the word and I will be there for you ALWAYS.

Embodiment
(McDowells)

We met by way of occupation. My flamboyantly arrogant demeanor and my word choices at the time were probably less than savory. Over time, I got to know you more and more, you gently smiling and taking the harsh jokes as a result of light workplace hazing. But there was always something more to you. Just beneath the surface of a government issued shell was a man with a ginormous harnessing of power. One day while working together the question of spirituality was a hard line that we started to discuss. I quickly vented my frustrations of the corporate church to him and he just nodded his head in what appeared to be in agreement. If I only knew what he was really holding back from speaking. Out of love and a situational impulse, I married my second wife. I had asked "J" if he would do me the honor of marrying us at the state capitol building. "It would be an honor" he said, "but I don't think my ordination is acceptable to the state." Who knows what the true reasons were…but like he's done several times to me, his gift of foresight is second to none….he even predicted the next Presidency with pure accuracy. We had our reception later that year and he and his family attended. I remember putting him on the spot to ask the blessing over the food that we were serving amongst a pretty good-sized crowd….he did it with no equivocation. Over time, I started experiencing horrible/disgusting acts from whom I loved most in this world. I was an emotional wreck and was completely lost. I begged him to pray for me, her and our marriage right there in the workplace. He did…and so did his wife. I can't explain to you the immense power these two have with their

God. It's something that I have rarely seen in my lifetime but has yielded the biggest results I have ever seen. Like most people, the intensity of prayer may fizzle out over time. I asked "J" one day if he thought I was praying wrong. He laughed in typical "J" fashion and explained to me that I already knew how to pray but just wasn't paying attention to what. He was the first to teach me about what God's will really is. He and his wife showed me how to observe and to pray for understanding. On that day, my spiritual journey as a Christian really took flight. I stopped asking for specifics and started praying for the will of God…it changed everything. "God heard you the first time…you don't have to lament to him the same things over and over and over. Tell him your concerns, ask for his will in it….and watch what happens." Such a simple concept…but one that changed everything for me. I'm not here to be a cheerleader for the church. Yes, I am a Christian but I'm not going to play "perfect" or be over-zealous or even try to force-feed or "sell" you on what I believe. Just like some of you have no faith system, perhaps you are a staunch Atheist…it doesn't matter. We can mutually respect each other's belief systems and have philosophical conversations on a mature level. "J" and his wife "C" (yes…some of you also) are the true embodiment of Christ to me. The selfless givers who will stay up late to engage with the spiritual realm to settle your heart and mind….who stop at nothing to ensure you feel loved. This is a testament to humanity…even more so a testament to a faith-based family who truly understand what "selfless" means.

FROM RICHES TO RAGS

Funny how the faulty threads in our life's tapestry seem to catch our attention, more than the grand design. Are we seeking perfection? Have we not accepted our imperfections? Every string is a crucial part of the story. Anyone with a beating heart has had their share of snags and tares in life. With that – more than imperfection, it's character. Though my tapestry is more a patchwork than a thread-scape, it's a beautiful/vivid display of sewn tragedy mixed with miracles and love. No one expecting a masterpiece would display it with a boastful mouth. But, a person seeking comfort and warmth will gain the most while wrapped up in it.

Letter to my Younger Self

You know nothing of the life you're about to live. There will be times where you'll think "I can't seem to escape the things that have hurt me." Young man, you will be forged in hurt. Your confidence in who you are will be destroyed many, many times. You will put your trust in so many beautiful women that will eventually jade you to ruin. "At this point, why go on?" you'd ask the older you. Because the essence of who you truly are as a man will have you sitting faceless amongst kings. Your passion will be known around the world and your influence will reach the crevices of darkness for those who need you the most. You will pride yourself in being selfless. You will champion for those who cannot help themselves. You will be admired for your thoughts and people will follow your leadership to the ends of the earth. Know that purity will never exist because the living conditions among us are too harsh. However, you'll be a romantic believer in humanity and the wonders of the heart. You will mourn losses so much worse than death but you will choose to grow from the soot left behind. Your children will overwhelm you with joy – but the distance between you all will leave you restless. You will dance with death for decades but this will be the water that revives you. More and more, your desire to become a ghost will rise within you. That if you choose to speak to a total stranger, your impact will leave them suspended in positive thought for days. You have never been and never will be normal. You have always been the antithesis of it. Never fight that inner feeling of being exactly "who" you are, "when" you are, "where" you are. Fight your demons with brute force –

seeking only the will of the divine – that which the seed has been planted within you since you began breathing. Maintain the image of mystery that you will be subliminally famous for. Shake hands with your enemies and look them directly in the eye as if to say "You are nothing more than a nail…and I'm a hammer." Be savage in your journey of seeking truth. However, harm no one in the process if it can be avoided. Pity the jesters around you but accept them for who they are. Expose the liars and be the inertia for their change of cycles. Most of all, love yourself learn the truest definition of it (love) and in doing so, radiate that love to all. Grow daily – push forward boy and thrive!

Love Always,

You

Benjamin would like to sincerely thank the following:

To my God in heaven – you've seen me through the darkest corners of my life and without you present, I would not have survived. Thank you for your will and the understanding we have of each other.

Blaine and June Wilber, the Wilber family, "Pop," the Hensley family, Phil and Shawn, Todd Hale, George Vavold, Patrick Mee, Jason K. Martin, NNU family, the Bailey family, Doug and Julie Roberts, Deer Flat peeps, Don and Tina King, Adrian and Patrick Ryan, Noah Henson, Michael Wittig, Lester Estelle Jr., Lester and Patricia Estelle, Michael and Mary Rochelle, Bryan Kennard, Rudy Royball, Alan Butterfield, Anthony Marentic, Tony Labounty, Mark Lemy, Jason Mosely, Monica Alverado, Randall Hale, Jason Hanselman, Mike Tuttle, the Roberts family, Carrie Grant and family, Christopher Blessing, Damien Cirincione, Henry Lopez, Danielle Brown, Heather Fitzgerald, James Rapacon, Patrick Dansereau, Dylan Anitok, Jennifer Golden, Justin and Candice McDowell, Kimberley Locke, Tyrone and Erin Wells, Matt Hopper, Michael Irvin and family, Patricia Debor, Patrick Gray, Justin Skeesuck, Shila Jensen, Lipine Muraki, Kimo Muraki, Ken Roeder, Lauren Shaw, Seka and Chad, the Warren family, my fAMMOly, Alissa and Zachery Wilber, Tammi Francis, Bill Danielson, Chelsea Idicianni, Tim Klingenberg, E-Mac, Melanie and Absydee Slack, the Slack family. All the people who've contributed to these writing good or bad – may you find peace. To the countless others – Thank you!

www.ingramcontent.com/pod-product-compliance
Lightning Source LLC
Chambersburg PA
CBHW070814280726
48660CB00015B/625